Can I tell you about Anxiety?

Can I tell you about...?

The "Can I tell you about...?" series offers simple introductions to a range of limiting conditions and other issues that affect our lives. Friendly characters invite readers to learn about their experiences, the challenges they face, and how they would like to be helped and supported. These books serve as excellent starting points for family and classroom discussions.

Other subjects covered in the "Can I tell you about...?" series

ADHD

Adoption

Autism

Asperger Syndrome

Asthma

Cerebral Palsy

Dementia

Diabetes (Type 1)

Dyslexia

Dyspraxia

Epilepsy

ME/Chronic Fatigue Syndrome

OCD

Parkinson's Disease

Selective Mutism

Stammering/Stuttering

Tourette Syndrome

Can I tell you about Anxiety?

A guide for friends, family and professionals

LUCY WILLETTS AND POLLY WAITE
Illustrated by Kaiyee Tay

Jessica Kingsley *Publishers*
London and Philadelphia

First published in 2014
by Jessica Kingsley Publishers
73 Collier Street
London N1 9BE, UK
and
400 Market Street, Suite 400
Philadelphia, PA 19106, USA

www.jkp.com

Library of Congress Cataloging in Publication Data
A CIP catalog record for this book is available from the Library of Congress

British Library Cataloguing in Publication Data
A CIP catalogue record for this book is available from the British Library

ISBN 978 1 84905 527 7
eISBN 978 0 85700 967 8

6053 0051 08/15

Printed and bound in Great Britain by Bell and Bain Ltd, Glasgow

MIX
Paper from
responsible sources
FSC
www.fsc.org
FSC® C007785

Contents

"Hi my name is Megan and I am 10 years old. I worry and feel anxious about a lot of things. I thought you might like to hear about it as this might be a problem for you too."

"Anxiety is when you feel scared or worried about something and think something bad is going to happen. People can feel worried about all sorts of things, like what other people think of them, performing in front of other people, friendships, school, tests, their health, family, being away from their parents, the dark, injections, spiders and dogs. As you can see, people can feel anxious about anything really.

Everyone, children, teenagers and adults, gets anxious, nervous, scared or worried sometimes and this is completely normal. It might be hard to believe but sometimes it can be a good thing! Imagine walking across the road and seeing a car coming really fast. You would feel scared wouldn't you? Your brain would tell your body to get out of the way quickly and you would run across the road. That's a good thing as your anxiety stopped you from getting run over."

"People can feel worried about all sorts of things, like what other people think of them and performing in front of other people, friendships, school, tests, their health, family, being away from their parents, the dark, injections, spiders and dogs."

"Lots of people get anxious and stressed before important tests or exams. This means you might work at bit harder to make sure that you do okay. When people have to perform in front of other people, maybe competing in a race or acting in a play, they normally get anxious beforehand. Their body pumps something called adrenaline around their body and it actually makes them perform better. So anxiety can be a good thing...

But sometimes we have too much anxiety. We think something bad is going to happen when it isn't. We start to avoid things that make us anxious. Our body starts to get lots of signs of anxiety – we can't sleep, we get stomach aches, we feel our heart pumping really fast, we get cross easily or we become really tired. This is when anxiety isn't helping us any more and gets in the way of things we want to do."

"Our body starts to get lots of signs of anxiety – we can't sleep, we get stomach aches, we feel our heart pumping really fast, we get cross easily or we become really tired."

"This is what has happened to me and now my anxiety really gets in the way of my life and the things I can do. I am not alone in this. About 1 in 10 of all children and young people has anxiety that gets in the way and bothers them. That is about 20 people just in my school! However, you don't always know when other people are anxious. Children who get anxious can often be quite quiet so other pupils and teachers may not notice. Sometimes people who mess about and are loud can be anxious too.

The good news is that you can do something about anxiety so it doesn't get in the way so much. Later on in this chapter I will tell you what you, your family and friends can do to help you feel less anxious and scared, for example, your mum or dad encouraging you to face your fears rather than avoid them."

"I worry that my friends
will stop liking me."

"There are a few different anxiety disorders. I have something called Generalised Anxiety Disorder or GAD and this means that I spend a lot of time worrying about many different things. I worry that I won't do well at school and I will get bad marks. I worry that my friends will stop liking me. I worry about being late for school and getting into trouble. Last week, I worried because I forgot my packed lunch one day and I had a project at school that I worried I wouldn't be able to do. I sometimes worry about things I see on the news. I worry there might be a flood or a terrorist attack where I live."

"I worry about being late for school and getting into trouble."

"When I start to worry, I just can't stop and find myself thinking 'what if' this happened or 'what if' that happened. Things go over and over in my head and the more I think about them, the more worried I get. I try to stop worrying but the worries just keep coming back. It is worse at night when I am trying to go to sleep, as I lie in bed and my head spins with all the thoughts. This stops me getting to sleep and makes me really tired and then I get really cross and grumpy with other people the next day. It also affects my concentration so I can't get on with my school work very well."

"People often have more than one anxiety disorder. I also have something called Separation Anxiety Disorder, where I worry that something bad will happen to my mum and dad when I am not with them. I am really scared they will have a car crash and they might die. Sometimes it is really hard to go to school because I worry about them when I am there. If they are late to pick me up after school, I start to panic. When we are at home, I find it hard to go upstairs on my own, especially in the evening when it is dark. I worry that someone might break into our house and hurt us and so when I am in bed at night and hear noises, I worry that it is a burglar and shout out for my mum or dad. When I was younger, I used to sleep with Mum and Dad if I woke up in the night. It can also make it difficult for my parents to go out without me and leave me with a babysitter and they get fed up with not being able to go out and do things without me. Sometimes I feel cross that I find it hard to go to friends' houses and can't go on sleepovers with my friends."

"I also have Social Anxiety Disorder, which means that I get really anxious in situations that involve other people. I have anxious thoughts about what they think of me and worry that they might think I am boring or stupid. I worry I might mess my words up or not know what to say. My lessons can be difficult because sometimes we have to answer a question in front of everyone. I hate it! Even worse, sometimes we have to read out loud in front of the rest of the class. That makes me really, really scared. Even just chatting to people is hard and this can make hanging out with other children really hard. I find it easier with my friends, but if I meet someone I don't know, I just clam up and don't know what to say. I find it really hard to go to parties as I don't know who will be there and worry that I will have to play party games, will get it wrong and everyone will laugh at me. It also means that I miss out on doing clubs or activities after school that I'd really like to do."

"Children and young people might be scared of certain animals, like dogs or spiders, of injections, being sick, the dentist, lifts, heights or the dark."

"There are other types of anxiety too. Some children and young people are scared of a particular thing. They might be scared of injections, being sick, the dentist, heights, the dark, lifts or certain animals (like spiders or dogs). If they are scared of lifts, they might be scared that they will get stuck in a lift and so will then try to avoid going in a lift by taking the stairs instead. If they are scared of dogs, they might worry that a dog will bite them and so avoid going near dogs or to the park. You might have heard of these types of anxieties, they are called Specific Phobias.

Other young people get scared when they are in a crowded place or somewhere where they are worried they won't be able to escape from, like a busy shopping centre, a classroom at school or a long car journey. If they can't escape they can have a lot of strong sensations in their body, like their heart beating really fast, feeling dizzy and a tight chest, which can be quite scary. This is called Panic Disorder. They can worry they might feel ill, faint or even die, and will do everything they can to get away and avoid going to these sorts of places. If people avoid going to lots of places, this is called Agoraphobia."

"I try to stay near my parents as much as I can, so I avoid going somewhere without them."

"Anxiety can make you feel really scared that something bad is going to happen and so you start to avoid doing things that make you anxious. I try to avoid lots of social situations, like parties or clubs out of school. I try to avoid answering a question in class by keeping my head down so that the teacher does not spot me! I try to stay near my parents as much as I can, so I avoid going anywhere without them. I can't avoid school but I cry when we get there sometimes and try and get my mum to stay for as long as possible.

As well as avoiding things, I try extra hard to make sure my worries don't come true. I work really hard and spend a lot of time on my work so I get good marks. In the morning, I make sure my mum is up and we leave early so I don't get to school late. I try to be really nice to my friends so that they like me. I look out for anything that could go wrong. I keep an eye out for the news so I know if there is anything dangerous happening near me. I like to know for certain how things are going to go and so I ask my mum and dad lots of questions, even though often they can't answer them. I ask them if they think I will get a good mark, if they think my friends like me and if they will be okay while I am at school. I really want them to reassure me that everything is going to be okay. Although I feel better for a while once they say everything is fine, often my worries come back again so I have to ask all over again. These are called safety behaviours – ways to try to keep yourself safe."

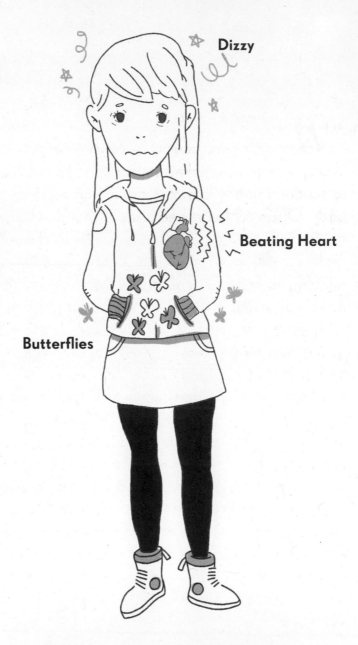

"Often my heart beats really fast, I feel dizzy, get butterflies in my stomach and feel sick."

"When I feel anxious a lot about things or am in a situation that makes me anxious, like going to school, I notice lots of things going on in my body. Often my heart beats really fast, I feel dizzy, get butterflies in my stomach and feel sick. I can't really concentrate on anything, as my head is just full of my anxious thoughts and, because I have trouble sleeping, I feel exhausted a lot of the time.

I argue with my mum and dad quite a bit as they get fed up when I don't want to go to bed at night and when I wake them up in the middle of the night. They worry that I will disturb my brother. They also get fed up when I try to get reassurance from them by asking lots of questions. They try to be patient, but when they are busy or tired, they end up just getting cross.

My mum and dad try to get me to do things, like speaking to people or going upstairs on my own, even though I feel really anxious. I can see why they want me to but sometimes they just don't understand how hard it is for me."

"Anxiety means I try to avoid answering questions or reading out loud."

"I find it hard to go to school because of my separation anxiety but I do go every day. Once I am in school, I carry on worrying about my mum and dad. I also worry about my work. This makes it hard for me to concentrate and I often don't understand what I need to do because I was thinking about a worry and not listening to the teacher.

I don't join in during class very much as I think people will think I am stupid. This means I try to avoid answering questions or reading out loud. I also don't ask for help if I need it, which means I can get stuck and not know what to do for ages.

I often spend ages on my homework even though I don't need to. I get cross with my mum when she says I have done enough as I am worried the teacher will tell me off for not doing a good job."

"I do go to play with my friends after school but I don't like to stay too long and worry about having to talk to their parents."

"At school, I find break-time hard as I worry I won't have anyone to play with. My friends are very nice to me but sometimes they want to play in a big group with other children who we don't know as well. I am too scared to join in and sometimes my friends get fed up when I just want to play with them. I sometimes ask them if they are cross with me, which I think they think is a bit strange.

I am lucky enough to have some really good friends. I have told them a bit about my worries and they try to help me but I am not sure if they understand it properly. I miss out on parties as I am often too scared to go. I do go to play with my friends after school but I don't like to stay too long and worry about having to talk to their parents. Although I would really like to go on sleepovers at my friends' houses, so far I haven't been able to."

"Having a sensitive personality is a really good thing because it means you are generally kind, caring and thoughtful."

"There are lots of different reasons why I, and other children and young people, have anxiety. For most of us, there is probably more than one thing that has caused it and keeps it going. Anxiety runs in families, which means that, in the same way you might inherit your mum or dad's eye or hair colour, they can also pass onto you parts of their personality. Children who get anxious are usually quite sensitive and may inherit this from one of their parents. Having a sensitive personality is a really good thing because it means you are generally kind, caring and thoughtful. The downside is that this can mean that you are more likely to develop anxiety. I know I am quite sensitive and my mum is too. If you do have anxiety, you might also notice that one of your parents or grandparents gets anxious about things too."

"Mum says that when she used to take me to netball club, I used to cry in the car on the way there (even though when I got there I often enjoyed it).

In the end, she said I didn't have to go, because she didn't like seeing me upset. The problem was I never got used to it and learned that I could cope."

"Some people think that if something difficult has happened to you in your life, you are more likely to be anxious (for example, if someone close to you dies, your parents split up or if you have to move schools) and that this might set off or trigger your anxiety. In general, this is only true if you are already more likely to become anxious by being a sensitive person, or if adults around you deal with the difficult situation in a particular way. There wasn't one thing that triggered my anxiety. I think I have probably had anxiety since I was very young – I can't remember ever not worrying!

We also learn a lot from our parents and other people we are close to. If we notice that someone is anxious about a particular thing and tries to avoid it, we might copy them. My friend's mum is scared of dogs and crosses the road when she sees one. My friend says she now does the same because she reckons her mum does it for a good reason.

Because our parents and families care about us they often try to protect us from getting upset. So they might let us avoid a situation because they know we will get anxious."

"Jo explained to us that lots of children have anxiety like me. She said that at the clinic, they see over 300 young people a year! She agreed with me and Mum and Dad that my anxiety was getting in the way and told me that the clinic would be able to help me to learn new ways of dealing with anxiety and would also help my mum and dad to learn the best ways to help me."

"My mum and dad talked to me and we agreed that my anxiety was really getting in the way of me being able to do things that I wanted to do. My mum made an appointment with the doctor, at our local GP surgery. My mum explained what was happening and the doctor referred me to a service that is especially for children and young people who have anxiety or other difficulties, called CAMHS (this stands for Child and Adolescent Mental Health Service).

I was really nervous about going there and was not sure that I would be able to talk to an adult who I'd never met before. However, I needn't have worried because the person who saw me and my parents was really nice. She was called Jo and was a Clinical Psychologist. After a while I felt more comfortable and was able to talk to her about what I worry and get anxious about. I even managed to talk to her on my own for a little bit. She asked me lots of questions and used a scale so I could show her how anxious I get in different situations. We also had to fill in quite a few questionnaires."

"Jo explained to us all that the most effective treatment for anxiety in children and young people (and adults too) is a talking therapy, called Cognitive Behavioural Therapy, or CBT for short. This involves working with a therapist who helps you learn new ways of dealing with anxiety. There has been lots of research that shows CBT works really well and so it is recommended that it is the best treatment for anxiety. CBT can be done in different ways, with the therapist meeting with just the young person, just their parent, in groups or even supporting the young person using a computer programme. Each way works just as well as the others. Sessions normally last around an hour and you have between 8 and 14 sessions."

"There are two main parts of CBT. The first part is the 'cognitive' bit. Cognitive means thoughts. CBT helps you to spot your anxious thoughts or worries and then to figure out if they are true or not. When we get anxious we often think about things in a way that isn't true. For example, when my mum is late to pick me up, I have an anxious thought that she must have been killed in a car crash. Anxious thoughts or worries make us feel anxious in the first place and are usually not true, so if we can change them into thoughts that are more likely to be true (which are often calmer thoughts), we will feel less anxious."

Date	Situation	Anxious thoughts	Evidence for	Evidence against
Tuesday 5th	Waiting for mum to pick me up from school	Mum has a car crash	She is late!	The traffic is busy at this time of day. My mum is a good driver. Someone would have phoned school if she had got hurt.

Megan's thought record

"During my CBT sessions with Jo, she asked me to keep a record of my anxious thoughts. Jo and I then looked at the evidence for my thoughts being true or not true. When we talked about my worry about Mum being in a car crash, I realised that when my mum is late it is more likely to be because she got stuck in traffic or was late leaving work. It really helped me to know that my thoughts are not facts, to think about whether my worries are realistic or not and try to come up with a new, more realistic thought. I use it lot when I am worried or in a scary situation.

The second part is the really important 'behavioural' bit. This relates to how the anxiety gets you to behave when you are anxious. As I mentioned earlier, when we are anxious, we behave in certain ways. We might avoid the thing that makes us anxious, be on the lookout for danger all the time, ask other people to reassure us that everything is okay or do other things to make sure our worries don't come true. All these things stop us from finding out what really happens. Do our anxious thoughts or worries come true or not? So, in CBT, you test out what happens if you change your behaviour. It's a bit like being a scientist doing an experiment. This means facing your fear rather than trying to avoid it."

		Anxiety Rating
Ultimate Goal :	To put my hand up and answer a question in front of the whole class	10
Step 6	To put my hand up in front of the whole class when my teacher has told me in advance what the question is so I know for sure I know the anwser	8
Step 5	To answer a question in a small group when we do group work	7
Step 4	To answer a question the teacher asks me when she comes over to my desk	6
Step 3	To go up to the teacher with two friends and ask a question	5
Step 2	To go up to the teacher at the front and ask a question (while everyone else is working)	4
Step 1	To ask the teacher a question when she comes over to my desk	2

Megan's step plan

"This can be hard to do so Jo and I designed a hierarchy (or step plan) for my fear about talking in class at school, so that I could face my fears, gradually starting with the easiest and moving towards the hardest. I rated how anxious I would feel (on a scale from 0–10) for each step so we knew what order to put them in. I started by asking the teacher a question when she came over to my desk and after a few weeks, managed to put my hand up in class and answer a question in front of everyone! I found out that the things I worried would happen didn't actually happen, and that it was a lot better than I thought it was going to be. Also, my mum rewarded me for doing each step, so this helped me feel motivated to do it. I have made really good progress with this and have done a lot of things I would have found too hard before. Now I have completed this hierarchy, we are going to make a new one for some of my other anxieties."

How family and friends can help

My mum or dad come to the first and last bit of my CBT sessions, so that they understand what Jo and I have been doing and what I am going to try out at home. It also helps them understand how the anxiety works and what they can do to support me when I am anxious.

Some things my family and friends can do to help are:

- Help build my confidence generally by encouraging me to be more independent.

- *Understand* that when I avoid doing things, it is because I am really anxious, not because I am being awkward, difficult or trying to get attention.

- *Stay calm* when I am anxious rather than get cross with me.

- *Ask me questions* to help me figure out for myself what I am worrying about and if my anxious thoughts are true or not, rather than reassuring me "it is fine" and telling me why I don't need to be scared.

- *Help me face my fears* very gradually by encouraging me and helping me to come up with opportunities to face my fears (e.g. ring my friend's mum to ask if I can come over to tea if she and I have decided that would be helpful for me to do).

- *Give me attention, praise or reward me* when I am brave and have a go at facing my fear, and not give me too much attention when I am anxious.

How my teachers can help me at school

Some things people at school can do to help are:

- *Meet regularly with my parents* and me to find out how my CBT is going and to share ideas about what we can do in school to help me.

- Help build my confidence generally by *giving me responsibilities* and jobs at school.

- To begin with, *let me leave the classroom* (or playground) and go to a place I feel comfortable in if I feel really scared.

- Help *distract me* when I am anxious. For example, have someone I can go to when Mum drops me off at school and help them with jobs so that I don't worry about leaving Mum so much.

- If I seem anxious, to *ask me* how I am feeling, what my anxious thoughts are and whether there is a more realistic way of thinking about it (rather than assume they know or rather than telling me it is okay).

- *Help me come up with and work through a hierarchy* for classroom situations I find scary so that we work towards me not leaving the classroom as things get easier.

- *Praise or reward me* when I am being brave and not give me too much attention for being worried or scared.

Other problems related to anxiety

The following problems are related to anxiety too. CBT also works well for these problems and is one of the recommended treatments for children and young people.

OBSESSIVE COMPULSIVE DISORDER (OCD)

OCD involves getting scary thoughts or pictures in your head that keep coming back and are hard to stop and/or having to do the same thing over and over again to stop bad things happening (like washing your hands a lot or checking things). There is another book in the series on this (*Can I tell you about OCD?*).

POST-TRAUMATIC STRESS DISORDER (PTSD)

PTSD is less common but happens if someone has seen or been involved in a traumatic event where they or someone else was harmed or seriously injured. People with PTSD get upsetting pictures, thoughts or nightmares about the event, get upset if they are reminded of the event, try to avoid things linked to the event and often have difficulties with sleep, concentrating and feeling jumpy or angry.

DEPRESSION

Some young people with anxiety go on to develop depression. You can also have depression without being anxious. Depression is feeling low and fed up almost all the time for at least two weeks. Young people with depression also have problems with sleeping, either not being able to sleep or sleeping too much of the time, and notice that they do not enjoy things as much as they used to. They also notice their appetite sometimes changes, that it is hard to concentrate and that they feel tired most of the time. Young people with depression also often feel hopeless and that they are no good.

Recommended reading, organisations and websites

BOOKS

Cain, B. and Smith-Moore, J.J. (1999) *I Don't Know Why...I Guess I Am Just Shy*. Washington, DC: Magination Press.

A book for 4–8-year-olds telling a story of how a boy overcomes shyness with tips and hints for parents.

Creswell, C. and Willetts, L. (2007) *Overcoming Your Child's Fears and Worries*. London: Constable Robinson.

This is a book for parents about how they can use CBT to help their anxious child or young person and includes lots of helpful strategies.

Creswell, C. and Willetts, L. (2007) *Overcoming Your Child's Shyness and Social Anxiety*. London: Constable Robinson.

This is a book for parents about how they can use CBT to help their shy or socially anxious child or young person and includes lots of helpful strategies.

Huebner, D. (2006) *What to Do When You Worry too Much: A Kid's Guide to Overcoming Anxiety*. Washington, DC: Magination Press.

This interactive self-help book has been written for children and parents and explains CBT techniques in an easy to understand way, with lots of pictures and metaphors.

Rapee, R., Wignall, A., Spence, S., Lyneham, H. and Cobham, V. (2008) *Helping Your Anxious Child*. Oakland, CA: New Harbinger Publications.

A book for parents using Cognitive Behavioural strategies.

Stallard, P. (2002) *Think Good, Feel Good. A Cognitive Behaviour Therapy Workbook for Children and Young People*. Chichester: Wiley-Blackwell.

A practical workbook for children and young people using CBT strategies.

Williams, M. (2000) *No Worries*. London: Walker Books.

A picture story book that promotes the idea that it is good to talk about worries, for children aged 4–8 years.

ORGANISATIONS AND WEBSITES

Anxiety UK
Zion Community Resource Centre
339 Stretford Road
Hulme
Manchester
M15 4ZY
Phone: 08444 775 774
Email: info@anxiety.org.uk
Website: www.anxietyuk.org.uk

Anxiety UK is a nationally registered charity that provides information, support and services to people with an anxiety disorder.

**British Association for Behaviour &
Cognitive Psychotherapies (BABCP)**
Imperial House
Hornby Street
Bury
BL9 5BN
Phone: 0161 705 4304
Email: babcp@babcp.com
Website: www.babcp.org.uk

The BABCP holds a register of accredited CBT therapists.

British Psychological Society (BPS)
St Andrews House
48 Princess Road East
Leicester
LE1 7DR
Phone: 0116 254 9568
Email: enquiries@bps.org.uk
Website: www.bps.org.uk

The BPS holds a register of Chartered Clinical and Counselling Psychologists who offer a range of therapeutic interventions.

Childline
NSPCC Weston House
42 Curtain Road
London
EC2A 3NH
Phone: 0800 1111
Website: www.childline.org.uk

Free helpline (online as well as telephone) for children and young people.

Royal College of Psychiatrists
21 Prescot Street
London
E1 8BB
Phone: 020 7235 2351
Email: reception@rcpsych.ac.uk
Website: www.rcpsych.ac.uk/expertadvice.aspx

Information and resources regarding a range of mental health problems including anxiety.

Young Minds
Suite 11, Baden Place
Crosby Row
London
SE1 1YW
Phone: 020 7089 5050
Parents Helpline: 0808 802 5544
Email: ymenquiries@youngminds.org.uk
Website: www.youngminds.org.uk

A national charity providing information and resources for parents, children and teachers regarding mental health problems.

USA

American Psychiatric Association
1000 Wilson Boulevard
Suite 1825
Arlington, VA 22209
Phone: 1-888-35-77924 1-703-907-
7300 if outside US or Canada
Email: apa@psych.org
Website: www.psych.org

Information and resources regarding a range of mental health problems including anxiety.

American Psychological Association
750 First Street, NE
Washington, DC 20002-4242
Phone: (800) 374-2721 or (202) 336-5500
Website: www.apa.org

Information and resources regarding a range of mental health problems including anxiety.

Anxiety and Depression Association of America
8701 Georgia Ave
Suite 412
Silver Spring, MD 20910
Phone: 240-485-1001
Email:
Website: www.adaa.org

Provides education, training and research for anxiety, OCD, PTSD, depression and related disorders.

Australia
Centre for Emotional Health – Australia
Building C3A, Level 7
Department of Psychology
Macquarie University
NSW 2109
Phone: (02) 9850 8711
Email: ehc.admin@mq.edu.au
Website: http://centreforemotionalhealth.com.au

Provides fact sheets on a range of mental health difficulties
in children.

Blank for your notes

Blank for your notes